T0193915

This Is My Story, This Is My Song

ROSHAN JAMES

WESTBOW
PRESS®
A DIVISION OF THOMAS NELSON
& ZONDERVAN

Scripture quotations marked (NIV) are taken from the Holy Bible, New
International Version®, NIV®. Copyright © 1973, 1978, 1984, 2011 by Biblica,
Inc.™ Used by permission of Zondervan. All rights reserved worldwide.

Scripture quotations taken from the New American Standard Bible® (NASB),
Copyright © 1960, 1962, 1963, 1968, 1971, 1972, 1973, 1975, 1977, 1995
by The Lockman Foundation.Used by permission. www.Lockman.org

This book is a work of non-fiction. Unless otherwise noted, the author
and the publisher make no explicit guarantees as to the accuracy of
the information contained in this book and in some cases, names of
people and places have been altered to protect their privacy.

WestBow Press books may be ordered through booksellers or by contacting:

WestBow Press
A Division of Thomas Nelson & Zondervan
1663 Liberty Drive
Bloomington, IN 47403
www.westbowpress.com
1 (866) 928-1240

Because of the dynamic nature of the Internet, any web addresses or
links contained in this book may have changed since publication and
may no longer be valid. The views expressed in this work are solely those
of the author and do not necessarily reflect the views of the publisher,
and the publisher hereby disclaims any responsibility for them.

Photo credit for images on pages 139, 141 and 143: Hilary Gauld-Camilleri

ISBN: 978-1-5127-7945-5 (sc)
ISBN: 978-1-5127-7946-2 (hc)
ISBN: 978-1-5127-7944-8 (e)

Library of Congress Control Number: 2017904156

Print information available on the last page.

WestBow Press rev. date: 05/19/2017

In memory of Grandpa, Granny,
Auntie Ann, Adrian's Granny, and Uncle Robin

Dedication

This book is a result of searching and finding purpose in a plan far greater than anything I could come up with.

To every seeking soul—may you find peace and love.

To my Norah and Theodore—may you find your life's purpose in faith. I love you both with all my heart. Thank you for teaching me how to be a mother.

Daddy and Norah picking apples at Uncle Josh
and Auntie Beth's farm. (Summer 2016)

Mom and Theodore walking the trail on the farm.
(Summer 2016)

"It is not fame that I desire, nor stature in my brother's eye. I pray it's said about my life, that I lived more to build Your name than mine."

Lyrics from "The Cause of Christ"[1]

<hr>

[1] Carnes, K.J., Hastings, B., and Fowler, B. *The Garden* (Brentwood: Capitol Christian Music Group, 2016). "The Cause of Christ."

Acknowledgements

To my late Grandpa Mark – Thank you for teaching me how to paint with brushes and words, and how to serve.

To my late Granny Rekha – Thank you for teaching me how to pray and give.

Mom and Daddy – Thank you for never giving up on me, and for praying for me every single day. I felt it and He heard it.

Josh and Beth – Where do I even start. Thank you for always loving and understanding me. Thank you for teaching me how to be a big sister.

Patrick LaFrenere – Thank you for teaching me to trust and love again. Thank you for loving me unconditionally before I could even see it. Thank you for being my partner in life, music, art, and poetry—everything. Thank you for what is still to come. I love you with all of me. You are a very specific answer to prayer.

Jimmy, Kim, Maddy, and Alex – You took me in so many times, I've lost count. Thank you for feeding me and for always looking out for me. Thank you for being an extended family for the kids and I. You are part of this healing process in countless ways and I love you.

Steven Ira – Thank you for being a remarkable co-parent. It is an honour to raise our little ones with you, as a team. I'm grateful we've been able to preserve and grow our friendship.

Amy, Jason, Ryan, Shannon, and Braydon – Granny and Grandpa's faithfulness lives on through each of you. May you continue to pursue the face of God, and keep Him at the core of our family's purpose. This is our familial bond that can never be broken.

Uncle Steven, Auntie Karin, Uncle Merlin, Auntie Carole, my late Uncle Robin, and Auntie Patricia – You are and will continue to be warriors in the faith, through your prayers and your acts of love. Thank you for helping to raise the next generation of believers in our family.

Uncle Merlin – You were the only person who came to mind when I realized I needed someone to write an afterword for this compilation. In the decades of serving as a professor and a pastor, and with all your academic achievements, what stands out to me most is your humble nature and heart for God. Thank you for your spiritual leadership, and for entrusting me with your prayer requests.

Jones family – You took in an orphan who turned out to be my Grandpa. What else is there to be said about the incredible power of love and its impact, generation after generation. To each uncle, auntie, and cousin—please continue to use your love and unique gifts to serve others.

The entire James crew – My goodness, there are so many of us! Walk strong, each of you. We were built with hearts of courage and an unparalleled feistiness. Draw from those gifts to stay

grounded in the faith. Mallika, don't stop believing in each of us. Your love will be rewarded greatly.

Morgan, Alex, and Evan – I love you guys. Our childhood friendship is the backdrop for many of my best memories. Even though we don't get to see each other as much as we'd like to now that we've been allowed into adulthood, you will always hold a special place in my heart.

Cathryn and Mary-Jo – My sisters, we've gotten older, but I still feel like it was just yesterday that Mary-Jo and I met at Pioneer Girls, and then introduced me to Cathryn before the three of us started grade nine together. I admire and respect your steadiness, and that you never judged your wild-hearted friend through all the years filled with my head-shaking choices.

Jacqueline O'Hara – Lady, I love you and you are a gift to me–an inspiration of grace and patience. You were with me through some of my darkest times and I will never forget that.

Lysh, Becks, Christine, Kirby, and Kim – Ladies, this group of ours is important. A nucleus of trust and support within our beautiful community. May we continue to cheer each other on through everything.

Jeff Darroch – Thank you for always affirming my gifts, even when I thought there wasn't much of anything to use. Your life speaks unconditional love on a daily basis through your support for everyone who is blessed to call you a friend and brother, and through your dedication to service in action for those in need in our community. I'm thankful we've been able to deepen our friendship, and I look forward to sharing more with you.

Lena – Our heart-to-heart talks are a highlight of my week. I thank God for your sweetness, faithfulness, and insightfulness. It is beautiful to see your joy in the Lord, and how you boldly seek Him in all areas of your life.

Natascha Steckel – My spiritually-gifted friend, your experiences and insights have shaped and broadened my understanding of faith, angels, dreams and the Creator of all things. Thank you for your openness in our conversations, and for sharing your energy and time with me.

Grace Ibrahima, also known as "Amazing Grace" – We've known each other for a relatively short time in person, and a very long time in spirit and purpose. Without a doubt, the story of your life is a roadmap of God's mercy, and He's using you to reach people in life-changing ways. For the thirsty and the hungry in mind, body and soul, your story is good food and a stream of fresh water.

Inspiring Minds Early Learning Centre – Krista Schott, Faye Jantzi, and all the IM teachers – Thank you for diligently taking care of Norah and Theodore over the years, and for making their introduction to learning a warm, safe, and meaningful experience. From potty training, to bumps and scrapes, to dance parties, and rolling in the mud–we are indebted to you for supporting our children, our families, our community, and our unique needs on every level.

Friends from Queen's University in Kingston to Freedomize in Toronto – I ask for your forgiveness in that I was a slow learner. Some of you knew me at dark points in my story. I apologize and hope you're all continuing to walk in Christ as strongly as you did when we were in touch. I miss each of you. If we're still in touch

through social media, please know how grateful I am, and that I see even the most tenuous connection as a gift.

Women of Wellesley – You knit our community together with your support for one another. Thanks to Kathryn McEwin for starting this group which has become, and will hopefully continue to be, a rich resource for our beautiful village.

Eric Schroeder, WestBow Press – Thank you for not saying no. I learned so much through our conversations and look forward to more.

Reggie Adams, WestBow Press – Thank you for your patience, diligence and organization.

"Story of a stream" – photo taken just outside
of Wellesley, Ontario, Canada

Introduction

It's been a wild ride, my friends. A wild, thirty-six-and-a-half-year ride with no signs of slowing down.

For those of you who don't know, I've struggled with anxiety and bouts of depression for most of my life. I also dealt with eating disorders through my twenties. I've been married and divorced more than once. I have had a stubborn, rebellious heart for as long as I've known myself. And I'm sure I've alienated more than a handful of people because of my inability to properly care for my friends and family members at various points in time.

I want to start with that because it's important to understand how completely and thoroughly my life could be seen as a disaster and why I've felt, at times, worthy of being shunned by more than a few people.

In many ways, I am the woman at the well.[2]

However, that's not the whole story and it's far from the end. I'm learning that my worth is far greater than my history. My worth is not my past; nor is it the sum of my best-intentioned-yet-inevitably-broken choices. My value is in the hands of the One

---

[2] John 4:1–42 (New American Standard Bible).

who heals me – the One who held my hand even when I wanted to let go and run as far away as I could.

And I did run.

Still, He didn't let go.

With all my imperfect responses to a world of disappointment and heartache, my Creator faithfully reminds me every day I am His, and He draws me back to His place of grace, mercy, forgiveness and peace. He is a good Father and placed me in the right family and among the right people—my dedicated, spirit-filled grandparents Mark and Rekha Jones, my parents, my brother and sister-in-law, and many beautiful people who have blessed me with their wisdom, as well as opportunities to learn and grow. I also have the best children in the whole world and will happily debate anyone on that point. They are brilliant—wonderfully made, and I can take very little credit for that.

Despite the train wreck I described earlier, I managed to carve out a solid career, achieved success as an entrepreneur in my early thirties, and collected a long list of accomplishments from a professional and creative perspective. Please understand, though, I share this not to boast. I want to bring this to light in order to make the point that success is superficial and trivial when your insides feel like a constant battlefield.

Why Poetry?

I started writing poetry almost right after I learned how to string letters into words and words into sentences. I wrote about everything—nature, stars, the moon, the sun, animals, flowers, love. So much about love. So many lovesick poems penned from my childhood bed. In retrospect, I see now there was always a gap I was trying to fill with the idea of romance. After going through a season of heartache and this time—the only time—being driven to my knees in prayer in the most literal way, I finally started a process of healing so complete, all-encompassing, and immediate that my only language for describing it and responding to it was poetry.

Poetry is a powerful medium. It invites the reader to stay and sit awhile. It is layered, nuanced, and open to interpretation. It is lyrical while allowing the reader to bring their own melody. I enjoy the process of contemplation required in writing poetry almost as much as I enjoy reading others' responses.

My hope is that this compilation of poetry, scripture, lyrics, and images helps even one other wanderlusting life traveler—whether you think you're lost, seeking, or somewhere else on your journey. Very specifically, I want to connect with you if you're looking for encouragement or trying to make sense of your purpose. While I

knew a lot about Christianity growing up in church, and though I even professed at times in my life to be a follower of Christ, I was only ever at best one foot in. I know now from experience that doesn't work. It is shaky ground. It is the house built on sand that Matthew wrote about so wisely.[3]

In this book are my poetic responses to the healing I've experienced in my life as I seek to know more of God, and as I become familiar with His face, His voice, and His purpose for my life. If you feel a tugging on your heart to know more about *something*, but you're not sure what that *something* may be, or if you're trying to make sense of a faith you've carried for awhile but feel disconnected from belief, or if you simply enjoy reading poetry, I'm writing this with you in mind.

From one perfectly imperfect creation to another, may you find whatever it is you're seeking, and in seeking, may you find peace.

Roshan

---

[3] Matthew 7:24–27 (New International Version).

Blessed assurance, Jesus is mine!
Oh, what a foretaste of glory divine!
Heir of salvation, purchase of God,
Born of His Spirit, washed in His blood.

This is my story, this is my song...[4]

[4] Crosby, F. J. (1873). "Blessed Assurance."

at the start

somewhere deep
at the start of everything
morning light whispers
weightless
across always-night
calling our voices, trembling
into song

choose

and one day it's a bit brighter
and one day you choose
to live in the Light

seek

seek and seek more
into the edgeless everlasting

For we walk by faith, not by sight.

(2 Corinthians 5:7 NASB)

shatter my vision

lay waste to my doubting eyes

let my blindness be the emptiness

You fill completely with Your sight

return from stone

when you're swallowed up, fighting for air
when loneliness echoes off the walls
even when warmth starts to find your bones
and your eyes, your eyes, they return from stone
breathe into the relief, trace the carvings left behind
and remember
it's all part of your story

pain strikes like the lighting of a match
flaring into a new awareness
and burning into appreciation
for the smouldering old words
of faith, hope and love

no longer mine

in pieces
scattered
lay the cracked
and storm-shattered
days I couldn't let go,
so I held them,
close,
though my hands
bled
carrying the shards
of these moments
lost
and returned
from death
not meant for me,
and I put each piece down
at the place
where my feet couldn't walk,
where I no longer
longed to carry
what was no longer mine

Where I end
You meet

over

soften me over and over time,
a pebble between Your fingers

both

it isn't easy
but necessary
to consider both dark and light
to feel the balance
and shifting

to let one sink as a stone in deep water
and with the other, set our lives on fire

kindly break me again

and let's make forgiveness count this time

i want my feet to remember

each edge, piercing

each step, a lesson

toward mercy

beauty

the beauty in my broken hands
is their emptiness of that which
i no longer carry

bloom

and the desert of your heart
will start to bloom, watered by
Love's living rain

close my wounds,
but gently, please,
they're part of me
and leave
the darkest scars,
a remembered
story, of how
i broke, and how
i lived

garden

may my heart
be a garden
of forgiveness

heart in flight

shooting beyond the shadows
of what might've been
there's unfinished business
in these hollow-caged bones
and I get lost
in the forests of fine time
passing impatiently
a heart taking flight
with dust on my shoes
closing the distance
in growing devotion
waiting, waiting
to come home

closing in

i lay my soul bare
before the One who
redeems me
in spite of myself
He holds me, faithfully

in love, He brings me
to the place
where His plans
call me forward
gracing my horizon
pulling me
closer

though weak in the knees
He draws me in
nearer
with each step, side-by-side
we talk even
clearer

i know this is it
the prize is ahead
praise and honour
Lord of glory
i'm closing in

MY HEART TREMBLES
TO MY KNEES, SHAKING
IN RELIEF
AND FROM OVERCOMING
DISBELIEF
LOOKING INTO THE FACE OF
UNDESERVED LOVE
AND BREATHING IN
A GRATEFUL REALIZATION
NOTHING WILL BE THE SAME

go gently

bold heart, go gently
though you beat with resolve
walk peaceful
even with the war
of flesh and spirit on your back
deal softly
with the hardened and the seeking alike
they may be the same

survival songs

i reached the shore
and wrapped myself
in a blanket of survival songs
smoky and warm
from the stubbornly-smouldering fire
of the faithful
who've come before

Now faith is the assurance of things hoped for, the conviction of things not seen.

(Hebrews 11:1 NASB)

unseen

in things unseen
we find the rising of tomorrow

thirst

You waited
through all my desert-dwelling years
knowing i would thirst for You
the rest of my days

We grow in these places
Where we heal
But first, we must break
And befriend loss
In those same places
Where ego and comfort
Spend their idle time
Convincing us
We're good where we are

steal

break in
steal my old ways
blessed thief
take
my everyday's
demons
of complacency and pride
make room
for unbrokenness
promised
and planned
fullfill and complete
Your humble servant

'who am I?'
is the question
each generation
asks of itself
of each self
in the ongoing search
for the meaning
of this moment
successors in a faith
a tradition traded
for authentic and original living
from an ancient beginning
deepening
desiring to know
more

this

i have walked the world over
to know with certainty
there is no greater Love
than this

safe

You are the safe-keeper
of my soul's oldest secrets

Come to me, all you who are weary and burdened, and I will give you rest.

(Matthew 11:28 NIV)

call

i call to You
long, through the night
and, in You, find rest
each morning

centre

stand, look
you can see how it all works together

One body
One heart

the earth, it beats and breathes and wakes and walks

a living jewel

Life, at the centre of the universe

quiet

my heart holds
a quiet place
for You

in

in Your presence
i'm at peace

rain

speak to me as rain
whispering into
a flower's thirst

wait

rely on
the wait
and trust
the response

gain

let us move forward
with more wisdom gained
through each loss

calmed

Your storm-calming words
quiet my thunderstruck heart

clear

i breathe and breathe
as the smoke clears
pulling into my lungs
the life You spoke
into being for me

complete

we will find completion
of death and rebirth
wherever we open our hearts

extend

in the same way
the universe holds space
for each star
and the earth, each tree
so too, Your Love expands
and extends to each soul

no end

when Love wins the battle
over a doubting heart
there is no need for fear
and no end to peace

Weeping may last for the night,
But a shout of joy *comes* in the morning.

(Psalm 30:5 NASB)

You are my
morning
of *joy*

Afterword

When Roshan requested me to write the afterword for *This Is my story, this is my song*, I felt both humbled and honoured. Being my favorite niece I could neither refuse her nor resist my opportunity and privilege to have a little part in her beautiful story. Her life's journey for 36.5 years can be summed up in two words, 'Amazing Grace'. Gifted by God to express her experiences from her heart in poetry, Roshan shares a past 'wild ride' where success was superficial and romance hollow. True, pure, and genuine love that every human heart yearns for is found only in an intimate, deep, and 'face-to-face' relationship with the epitome of love – God, found in the greatest love story, the Bible. This is the love of Calvary that Roshan rediscovered on her knees. Every saint has a past, every sinner has a future. *This is my story, this is my song* expresses this truth in a heart-to-heart poetic language. Interspersed with beautiful photographs (a picture is worth a thousand words) this tome is written as a testimony that there is hope for every reader who is desperately seeking for true love and purpose for living. That hope is in Christ alone.

Roshan and I commend our Savior to you.

Merlin Jones, Ph.D.
Professor Emeritus of Christian Theology and Ethics
Southern Asia Bible College

About the author

Roshan James is a business consultant, poet, runner and mom, among other titles. She lives in rural southwestern Ontario, Canada, in the village of Wellesley, with her two young children. Roshan's writing is an expression of her journey from faith to uncertainty and back, and it's also a way for her to process the craziness of life and the complexity of relationships. She derives inspiration from Biblical scripture, music, the natural world, philosophy, science and the simplest of interactions and details from everyday life. She looks for ways to connect all of this with themes of love, hope, time and purpose – transposing the minutiae into messages of healing and personal growth through faith. Roshan holds an Honours Bachelor of Arts degree in English Literature from York University, *summa cum laude.*

www.roshanjames.com
facebook.com/poetrybyroshan
instagram.com/roshan_james

Printed in the United States
by Bookmasters

Printed in the United States
By Bookmasters